Endorsements

"Tender and true and beautifully written."
Stephanie Butland – author of 'Found in a Bookshop'

In Search of Lost Glitter is a beautiful mosaic that expresses the ebb and flow of grief in a visceral and authentic way. Skilfully crafted, the fragments of life shared through the snap-shots of short stories coalesce to form a vivid picture of a person dealing with loss in a real and personal way that not only informs, but also invites you in. This book offers a loving embrace to those who have experienced grief as well as gives insight into the less talked about areas of life that we all shall face.
Matt McChlery – author of 'Standing in the Storm: Living with faith and Cancer'

"Sarah has dealt with potentially heavy subject-matter – young widowhood, cancer, and the loss of her Dad – with a light touch and sprinkles of humour, giving the reader plenty of space to breathe and reflect. I felt like I had spent a lovely weekend holed up somewhere cosy with her, listening to her stories and getting a real sense of her relationships, and hopes for the future. In particular her honesty about mental health and difficult times is refreshing – it would have been so easy to have fallen into the trap of trying to be 'inspiring' non-stop."
Helen Anderson – author of 'Sagrada Familia'

"I read the first few lines and I was hooked. This is a powerfully written memoir, poured out from the heart. Taking the form of short stories, the book makes you feel like a fellow traveller through significant periods of Sarah's life - the good times, the hard times and the tragedy. Sarah writes so authentically that I felt I was right there with her, witnessing her heartbreak and sharing in her times of joy. This is compelling reading for anyone dealing with grief or wanting to help someone who is going through such hard times."
Lisa Goodridge (Ellie Carter) – author of 'All Saints'

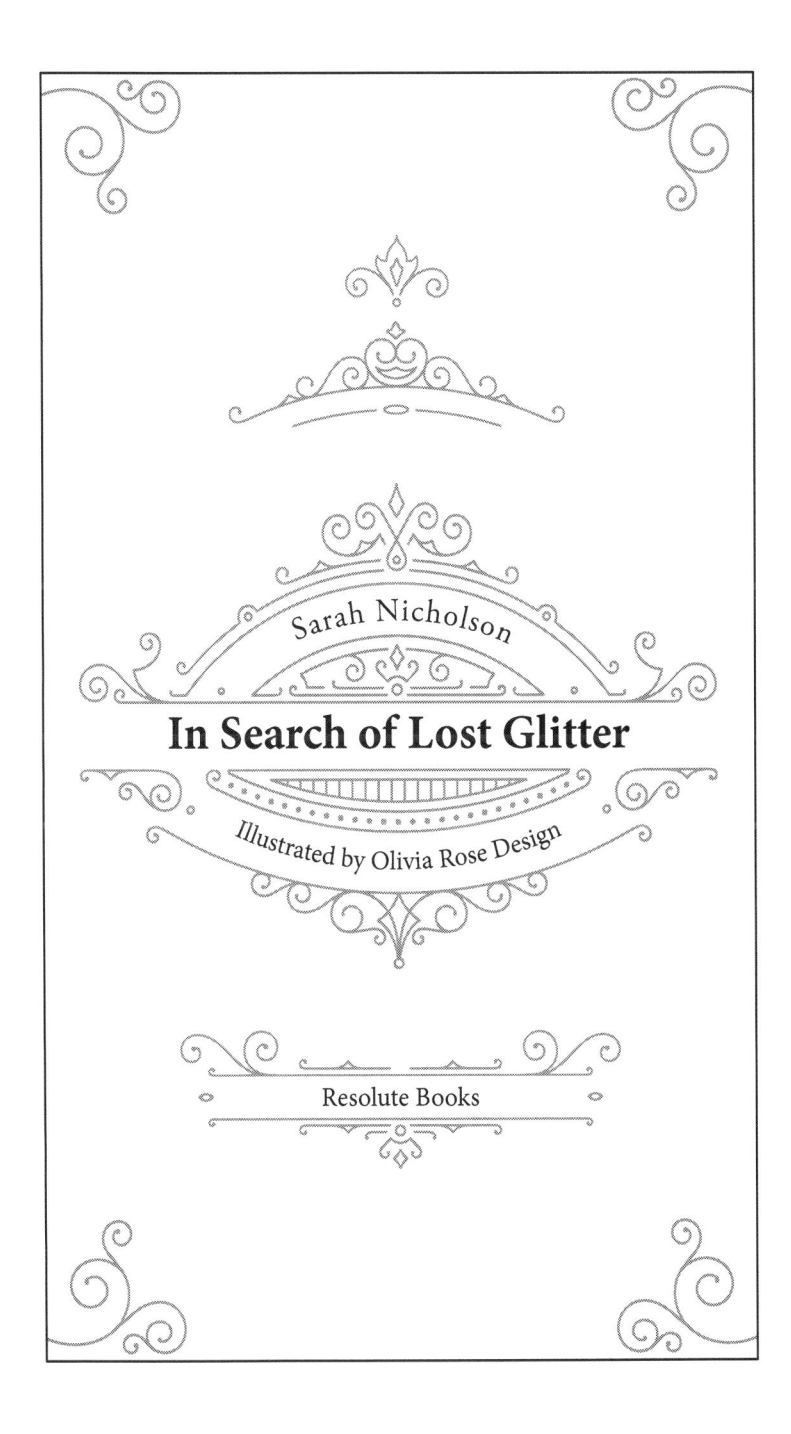

Sarah Nicholson

In Search of Lost Glitter

Illustrated by Olivia Rose Design

Resolute Books

Copyright © Sarah Nicholson 2024

The right of Sarah Nicholson to be identified as the author of this work has been asserted by her in accordance with the Copyright, Designs and Patents Act 1988.

All rights reserved. No part of this publication may be reproduced or transmitted in any form or by any means, electronic or mechanical, including photocopy, recording, or any information storage and retrieval system, without permission in writing from the publisher.

Cover design and illustrations by Olivia Rose Design
Typeset by Liz Carter (Capstone Publishing Services)

Second Date and *Anniversary Morning* were originally published online by Five Minutes (fiveminutelit.com)

Published by Resolute Books
www.resolutebooks.co.uk

Most people have deliberately not been named in this book and some names have been changed for the sake of anonymity.

When my husband died it was often the tiny details
that stirred up the most significant memories.
The colour of the top I wore for the funeral,
the sound of matches rattling in his coat pocket,
eating sausages and chips for Christmas dinner.

These are the fragments of lost glitter.

For Joe and Ben,
who both share their dad's smile.

'glitter (noun) –
an expression of an emotion in a person's eyes.'

Is the emotion a forgotten memory
or some new discovered joy?
It doesn't matter which.
Just hold on to it.

To Janice
With sparkle + glitter
Sarah Nicholson xx

Contents

November 2010	3
Early Years	21
2011: New Year, New Routine	33
Life Lessons	43
True Love	57
From This Day Forward	71
For Better	81
For Worse	95
Till Death Do Us Part	105
Survival	121
Everything Changes	137

POSITIVE DISPLACEMENT PUMP

You always said you didn't have a heart, just a positive displacement pump.

I giggled, unsure what to make of you. I'd never heard a heart described in engineering terms. It made you sound robotic and unfeeling.

That was the persona you used to keep people out, but gradually you trusted me and let me see your softer side.

I always loved to hear your strong and steady heartbeat as we lay together. I marvelled at the way we were two separate people and yet together we made a whole entity.

Until you died – unexpectedly.

Cause of death

a) Ischaemic Heart Disease

b) Coronary Artery Atherosclerosis.

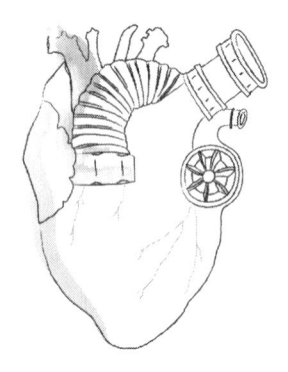

'What does that mean?' I asked a friend who was a GP. I didn't understand medical terms any better than the mechanical ones you used.

'In the simplest terms, it means a heart attack.'

Perhaps you would have called it a 'pump malfunction', but it was all the proof I needed that you had a heart after all.

November 2010

I STARTED A BLOG

Two weeks after Andrew died, on what would have been his forty-ninth birthday, I started a blog, Unravelling Edges, to help me work through my grief and stitch together what was broken.

I poured out my thoughts into cyberspace to keep me sane and process my fragile emotions.

I don't know how far my words reached, but close friends told me how helpful it was for them to understand what I was going through. I started to dream that my words could travel further, maybe a book deal, a movie – could I be a superstar on the back of grief? Could I end up on daytime TV, dispensing my curated wisdom with benevolence?

There had to be some good to come out of tragedy and I've always been a daydreamer, with my head in a cloud of sparkle.

Then there were times when I wondered if anyone cared about one woman's journey. So obscure and ordinary. I wasn't alone in this grief; I wasn't unique or special.

I wrote made up fictitious stories instead. Short ones I could finish in an afternoon, post online and wake up the next day to a handful of comments from friends around the globe. Until I grew tired of our little bubble and I put away my writing dreams and boxed up my ambitions.

But my real story grew with tendrils reaching in all directions. It still needed to be told. I needed to write it from beginning to end, for anyone that would listen.

With twelve years' worth of scattered words on my blog about grief, loss and putting the pieces back together, I foolishly thought it would be easy to write a memoir – oh, how pretentious! I planned a tidy romcom-style ending – an even more ridiculous notion. Instead, cancer happened, real life, more loss, even a global pandemic, for goodness' sake. We were heading for disaster movie territory.

What if I concentrated on the smaller, seemingly insignificant details of my life?

I set myself a challenge to write one hundred pieces of creative non-fiction, each one tightly crafted in only a hundred words. Stories of love and loss, fear and failing, being the odd one out and forging my own individual path despite everything.

Some stories remain one hundred words long and I love their neatness, like perfectly wrapped gifts tied with a bow, but life, and especially grief, isn't always so neat and tidy. Emotions cannot be contained; they spill out, often in the most inconvenient ways.

My story is not linear with a perfect fairy-tale ending but hopefully somewhere in the fragments is a bit of sparkle, a piece of lost glitter that catches your eye and brings some comfort, some hope, or a reassuring word that you are not alone in the heartache you are going through either.

FOUND DEAD

'Everything must be OK. No missed calls or texts.'

I stayed at my friend's an extra five, fifteen, thirty minutes? I lost track of time. But when I returned home, it was strangely quiet.

'Where's your dad?'

'Upstairs. He came down for the football results.'

When I went out, he was lying on the bed with a bad headache. I'd kissed him goodbye and he'd pulled away, wincing. He wasn't lying on the bed now.

The radio was on, he liked to listen to the news; I always found it too depressing.

I called his name but he never answered.

FIRST NIGHT

I stood by the Aga, absorbing its warmth.

Phone in hand I dialled the familiar number.

My words were matter-of-fact. 'Andrew died.'

I heard Mum drop the phone in shock. Dad took over on their end of the line as I repeated my words, which even I couldn't take in.

They hastily packed, forgoing their usual Saturday evening of playing cards, and arrived just before midnight.

I sat in the kitchen surrounded by a few friends, reminiscing, crying, even laughing.

The boys had long since gone to bed, youngest son opting to sleep with me. It was a comfort to finally climb into our big bed acutely aware of his small, warm body breathing softly beside me.

I couldn't sleep at all.

SLEEPLESS

I ran over the last few hours, over and over again.

Finding Andrew lying beside the bed, face down.

Jelly legs as I went downstairs to find my mobile phone and make the 999 call.

Turning Andrew's body over, seeing his face blotchy, his skin already cold to touch.

Oldest son, aged thirteen, doing chest compressions, hopeful that the gurgling noise was a sign of life.

Youngest son, only ten, waiting by the front door for the ambulance, being helpful.

The silly sign on the gate that said 'Beware of the Dogs', left by the previous owners, that we'd never taken down. None of the locals took notice of it, especially in conker season when they treated our garden as a park, but the paramedics stopped to ask the question: 'Are your dogs out?'

'We don't have a dog!' I almost screamed down the phone, aware time was ticking.

Being tasked with writing Andrew's personal details on a piece of paper, just for something to do, to keep me out of the way.

Calling a friend, who came and fed the boys and sliced up a pear for me, fanned out on a plate.

Everything seeming to take so long, there must be hope, then suddenly realising Andrew didn't even have pyjamas to wear in hospital, even for an emergency. I imagined presenting him with a bag from Marks and Spencer's when I went to visit and us laughing.

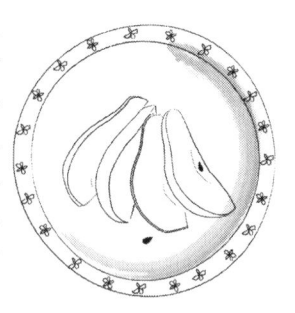

Eventually the news there was nothing else they could do.

Andrew was dead.

Sitting with the boys and telling them their dad had gone to be with Jesus in heaven… at least their years of Sunday school gave them a point of reference.

Phoning family, Andrew's, and mine, ours – Andrew is dead.

The first condolence phone call from our old vicar. 'You will come and do the funeral, won't you?'

Friends arriving, filling our cosy kitchen with love.

My parents arriving so late.

Going to bed but unable to sleep, thoughts going round and round.

A small child beside me, softly breathing, an odd lamp from another bedroom brought in to illuminate the patient – no, the deceased.

Andrew is dead.

Andrew is DEAD.

ANDREW is DEAD.

SIXTEEN YEARS, SIX MONTHS, SIX DAYS

Our marriage will never last any longer than that.

Others will reach anniversaries in silver and maybe even gold. I will celebrate with them, marvelling at the longevity of their relationships. Pondering, perhaps, would we have reached such milestones?

Years pass and eventually I realise I've lived in our forever home longer without you than with. Not long to go now until my widowhood outlasts our marriage.

Yet I am still 'Mrs' – a housewife without a husband. One day I will no longer be out of sync with my generation because in the end there are always more widows.

IN CASE OF AN EMERGENCY, USE THIS CARD

The card didn't have flowers on the front, no sentimental words inside expressing deepest sympathy. Every card and letter received was sent with love, but this was given with a deeper understanding. An acknowledgement that even the most eloquent of words cannot soothe a broken heart. Sometimes you need sharp, shouty, rude words. The card was not a proper condolence card but one that said 'Feck Off!' on it. Words to yell at grief, or perhaps words to say, if you dare, to those who overwhelm you when all you want is to be left alone, to learn to grieve.

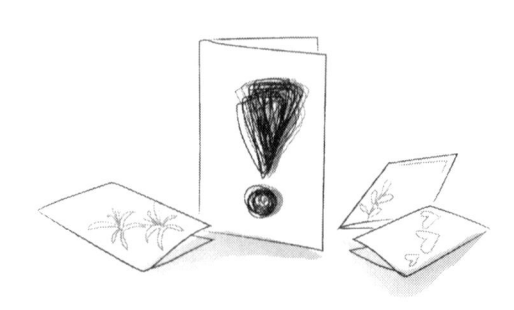

THE LAST KISS

Alone for one last time and you are still mine to touch.

I ruffle your hair, unusually brushed, far too tidy. The rip in your jeans is familiar, from a dog bite, I think. I stick my finger in to feel the solid muscle – or maybe it's rigor mortis?

Beneath your T-shirt I can hear the crinkling of a plastic bag, postmortem secrets I do not want to disturb.

Finally, our lips meet for our last kiss. Yours are arctic cold, not thawing at my touch. I cannot share my living breath and you have nothing left to give.

THE GREATEST 'WHAT TO WEAR?' DILEMMA

I wore the lilac top. 'Someone who loves you very much must have bought you that.' I could hear the gentle teasing of your voice acknowledging the gift you chose with great care, never once imagining I would wear it on such a sombre day as this.

Made from the softest cotton, it wrapped me in a tender embrace. My funeral skirt swirled, fully gathered with frills and lace; it was the only black item in my wardrobe.

Did we joke too much with our flippant plans? I gazed at my reflection.

'You look nice today!' I heard you say.

CREMATION FIRST (FAMILY ONLY)

No one carried you into the crematorium.

'You can push the coffin on the trolley,' said the undertaker, helpfully.

One brother, one nephew and our eldest son stepped forward, arranging themselves and taking their places beside you.

I felt youngest son extricate his small hand out of mine. At only ten years old he needed to play his part.

He wore a green zip-up hoody and red bow tie which he wanted specially made. It was before *Dr Who* made them cool, so I've no idea why he thought it appropriate.

My dad reached out for my redundant hand.

A MOST UNUSUAL CELEBRATION

'I want the cricket TV theme played at my funeral.'

'You hate cricket!'

'But it's such a jolly tune.'

Were you serious when you made such trivial plans?

For good measure I threw other favourite things into the service – the reading from our wedding, a specially written poem, the harp music you enjoyed, and our nephew on the saxophone. The vicar, a good friend, indulged the grieving widow. You would probably have been embarrassed by the display. It was a far longer funeral than it needed to be.

'When people leave, give everyone a Quality Street chocolate and play Perry Como "Magic Moments".'

Some chose the purple one because it was your favourite, others deliberately picked another. At least it was nearly Christmas and the big tubs were in plentiful supply.

I used to laugh at your crazy ideas, but I set each one in motion in your honour, your final wishes – fulfilled.

AN ABUNDANCE OF SNOW

Days after the funeral, winter arrived with decisive devastation. The whole country ground to a halt in a snow storm. It wrapped me in a beautiful blanket of stillness, my body already numb from grief rather than cold. I couldn't move on, I was frozen, nothing would ever be the same. Friends arrived by foot with bags of shopping, fresh milk, real butter. Puddles gathered underneath the wet hats and coats, steaming by the Aga. They brought a different kind of chaos, more beautiful than the sparkling snowflakes; they poured love and laughter into our home. A spark of life.

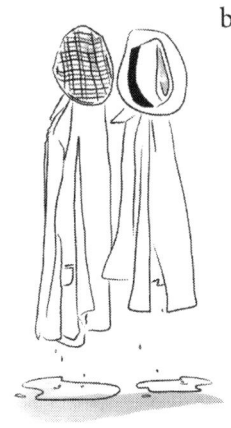

OVERPROTECTIVE

Youngest son was unimpressed as I fussed, fastening his coat properly to keep out the bitter cold. He pulled away sharply and I burst into tears.

He can't cope with my fragile emotions and deals with his own grief by shutting it out.

Picking up his school bag he shouted at me and slammed the front door.

He can walk to school by himself, he is nearly eleven, but since 'everything' happened I've been taking him halfway, glad of a walk in the snow.

I ring the school a bit later just to make sure he arrived safe and sound.

MAD WOMAN ALERT

The shopping whizzed by too fast.

'Can I have a minute to pack?' I pleaded, my voice at a reasonable level, but my protestations went unheeded, so I resorted to throwing items into my trolley, eager to be gone.

'Uh-oh!' commented a male customer under his breath. 'Mad woman alert!'

That was the final straw. I spun round and faced him. 'Mad woman who's just lost her husband!' My voice was raised, people stopped and stared, but no one offered assistance or asked if I was alright.

I pushed my trolley out of the shop and life carried on.

FIRST CHRISTMAS

The snow, which had abated in the middle of December, was back. The possibility of getting to my parents to celebrate Christmas was non-existent; I couldn't even get the car off the drive. My washing machine wasn't working because the pipes had frozen.

A decision was made. I called for a taxi, and we took one bag of presents and one of washing to my mother-in-law's. We had sausages and chips for Christmas dinner, it was a Saturday after all.

While the washing machine whirred, we opened presents, excessive and lavish maybe, to make up for all that was lost.

Early Years

BACK TO THE BEGINNING

Eventually in-between Christmas and New Year, the weather eased and we made it to my parents'.

Andrew always said I got louder as we drove along the A14 and crossed the border into Suffolk. It did fill me with glee to be 'coming home', in the same way that spying the distinctive Teesside landmark of Roseberry Topping, on our return trips, filled my heart with gladness.

Each of us has history, a place where we were born and our story began. A once-upon-a-time moment when life is full of endless possibilities and there's a childlike excitement of being in a place you feel you belong, somewhere that holds so many memories; a place where you feel secure and safe. You retreat to a time when life was simpler and you don't have all the grown-up responsibilities. A place where someone else can decide what to cook for tea.

MIXED MESSAGES

My mother told me I was born at Heath Road. As a small child whenever I heard the mention of Heathrow I got confused, but I know I was born in a hospital, not an airport! I landed fully formed, seven pounds, four ounces.

'You have a lovely daughter,' the nurse told my dad.

He grunted, 'A girl?' A man of few words, many of those were made up, or Suffolk sayings.

He was similarly unsure of what to say when asked 'Who gives this woman away?' at my wedding. Maybe by then he didn't want to give me up?

LIFE AND DEATH – A TRUE STORY OR FAMILY MYTH?

Two years after I was born, Mum was expecting again. How much I understood at such a tender age is debatable, but this is the story that's told of my brother's birth.

On the morning my dad drove Mum to the hospital, a dozy pheasant crossed the road. Dad didn't stop for the deceased, not when new life was eager to be born. He knew the law – you couldn't pick up a game bird you had killed, but you could pick up one you later 'found'.

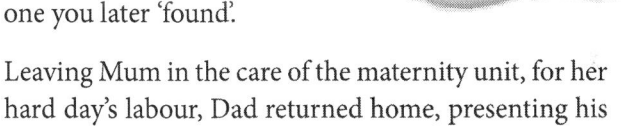

Leaving Mum in the care of the maternity unit, for her hard day's labour, Dad returned home, presenting his prize to my grandma before heading off for work.

Grandma, a butcher's wife, plucked and skinned the bird, making a casserole for our tea, while I played at her feet.

Well satisfied with his meal, Dad drove back for visiting time to see his son.

FIRST MEMORY

The carpet on the stairs had large flowers on it, one flower then two, one flower then two, yellow, red and blue, yellow, red and blue. There were seven steps, a turn and then another seven.

I was only two and a half, but I knew my colours and I could count. Today I was wearing my red dress and something special was happening, my brother's christening, but everyone would still make a fuss of me too.

I carefully reached the bottom and turned into the kitchen. There was Dad, smoking his pipe, and he smiled at his pretty girl.

SUCH A GOOD GIRL

Once upon a time my world was very small, my hair was plaited and my dresses handmade. I grew up believing everybody knew who I was and who I belonged to. Like his father before him, Dad was a respected local butcher, with spies everywhere. Then there was Grandma, a formidable role model with an even further reach of contacts in the depths of the church community. She believed her pew was hers alone; woe betide any stranger who sat there. Being 'such a good girl', I sat beside her and spent the service swapping hymn books with her when I found the number first.

DANCING GIRL – A STAR IS BORN

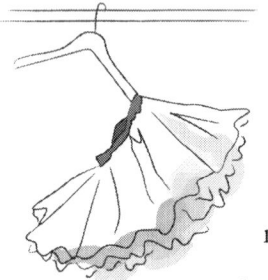

My first tutu was green, that delicious colour of envy, although at the age of five or six when I twirled on the stage with everyone watching me, there wasn't a jealous bone in my body.

After the show, my family reinforced the notion that I was the real star among the group. Sometimes I was picked for the solo parts, which was all the proof I needed.

Looking back, my only real regret is that I gave it all up too soon; my teenage years approached and I yearned for new horizons, but the desire for applause never faded.

CHILDHOOD FILTERS

I grew up thinking my nana was posh, because she had a fur coat. It was undoubtably fake. She lived with Grandad in a tiny terraced house, worked in a factory and smoked; you can't get much more working class than that. But they had luxuries we didn't – a car, a phone and a colour TV to watch the wrestling on a Saturday afternoon. To me this was the height of sophistication. At home we watched the snooker in black and white, used the phone box around the corner and Mum took us out by bus: 'One and two halves, please.'

MY PERSONAL MISSION

The tent mission came to town each summer, setting up the large marquee on the playing field behind the library. There were songs and stories and stickers; the more you collected, the better prize you could earn – perhaps a whole Bible instead of a set of Gospels.

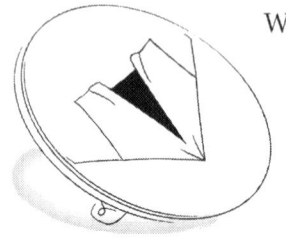

We wore our badges with pride at school, rebelliously turned upside down because then the tent symbol looked like a pair of knickers, appealing to our childish humour.

Each week there was a chance to perform, I put my name down to sing a solo – part of my personal mission to be a star.

ACCIDENTAL UNDERSTUDY

Most of the girls in my year were Joseph's brothers, a key part of the story. Dancing girl in Pharaoh's court was a made-up part. I only danced in one scene and then faded into the chorus-line.

Then one girl was ill on the first night.

I marched up to the teacher. 'Can I be a brother? I know all the words and what to do.' I can't believe I was bold enough to voice my opinion to a grown-up, but I knew an odd dancing girl was expendable.

The teacher said she would think about it and I remember being cross at her indecision. Perhaps she was as shocked as me at my audacity.

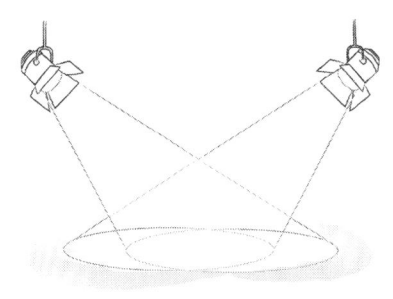

Later that day she came and found me; I could be a brother alongside my friends. But if I'm honest, the victory was bittersweet and I missed the dancing.

2011: New Year, New Routine

KITCHEN CALENDAR

Each January I would mark up the kitchen calendar with the dates Andrew would be working. Two weeks away on the oil rig, just under three weeks at home with us, allowing for travelling time and other adjustments.

I was thankful when we returned from my parents', in time for the start of term, that there was a new calendar on the wall without any such marks made. This was our new reality, with no rota to guide us.

No skipping forward to see if Andrew was home for school holidays, birthdays, or Christmas. He was away permanently now, never coming home.

There would be no bags left in the hallway, no trips to the station, no more counting the hours until a flight landed or praying for better weather when fog prevented him from leaving the rig.

The boys accepted only having one parent around for the two weeks away; I was always the stable one, solid and dependable. Two weeks was now forever.

Life would carry on. It had to.

JANUARY BLUES

Grief caught up with me in January. I'd tried to hide from my raw emotions by looking after other people, filling my days with Christmas preparation, writing the church Nativity, buying presents that nobody really needed.

January is such a bleak month and I suddenly realised Andrew wasn't on some extended work trip; this was my life now, full-time single parent.

One Sunday in church I shamelessly cried through the whole service, but most of my tears were private. I spent many afternoons lying on the sofa in tears, only drying my eyes in time for the school run, pulling myself together.

CREAM CAKES AND SYMPATHY

'It's worse losing a son than losing a husband.'

My mother-in-law dropped that bombshell into the conversation as we sat drinking tea and eating cream cakes, an established ritual after the weekly shop.

I'm sure her words are true; losing a child is not the way things should happen. We would like death to be tidy and ordered.

I could have replied with something spiteful. Instead I licked cream off my fingers and let her comment slide, aware we were both grieving the same person. We both carried regrets that we never shared because grief shouldn't be a competition.

MORTGAGE PAID

My hand was shaking as I opened yet another important-looking letter. Death certificates sent out in all directions were coming back to roost, details amended, 'sorry for your loss'.

This letter informed me the balance of the mortgage was now zero, but the cost of paying it off was too high.

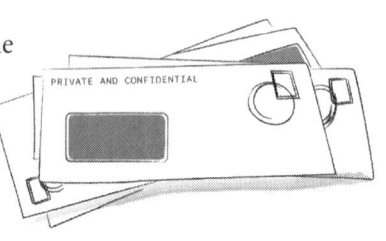

How you would have delighted in looking out of the window, surveying all your land. Not a blade of grass or single light fitting was owned by the bank.

Instead, I burst into tears at the huge responsibility. Every tree that might fall down, every waterpipe that might burst, every brick that might crumble was mine and mine alone.

TODAY I... WROTE A POEM THAT DOESN'T RHYME

Today I remembered to breathe.

I did one load of washing but left the ironing.

I fed the boys pasta for the third day in a row.

Last week I left the dishes in the sink and post unopened on the table.

I forgot to charge my phone and I was only 14p in credit.

The month before I couldn't do the crossword without you, and I woke up in a panic at ten to twelve, worried I hadn't locked the front door.

Six months ago, you were here to change the lightbulbs and shut the gate at night.

A SWEET SURPRISE

The first time I found a parcel on my doorstep it would have been our seventeenth wedding anniversary. Inside the carrier bag, a box of cream cakes, a sign of love and care dispensed by a benevolent angel of the parish. Other gifts were left on significant days, a hand-knitted shawl wrapped with some packets of love hearts, a beautiful mug I still use to this day for my tea. I eventually figured out who my gift-giving angel was, but we never mentioned it; both of us knowing broken hearts couldn't be mended with strawberry tarts alone.

RE-ROUTED

Six months after Andrew died, I decided to take the boys to Chicago to visit friends. It was a flight the three of us had made before, and we had had the most marvellous time. This was just what we needed.

But the boys squabbled over the window seat, although there was nothing to see but the Atlantic Ocean.

Meanwhile I squirmed, trying to get comfortable, my niggling back pain getting worse. The painkillers had worn off and I calculated it would be an hour before I could take any more.

Time was moving incredibly slowly.

We had been re-routed due to a volcanic eruption in Iceland, and when we landed for our unscheduled refuel, I wanted to cry, to scream, 'Let me off!' But we were stuck in these seats at the back of the plane by the toilets because I didn't have the foresight to check in early enough for better ones.

Within days of arriving, I realised I needed a break from the boys, not with them; being a full-time single parent was so hard.

I'd been widowed for six months and I truly believed my time for grieving was over. In reality, I barely understood what grief was.

What happened to me happens to people all the time. People die, it's a fact of life, but until you lose a loved one you have no idea how you will deal with it. Like most people who go through the shock of a sudden death, I was completely ill-prepared.

Six months after Andrew died, I put the house on the market. Everyone advised me against it because wisdom dictates you don't make BIG decisions in the first year, but I wouldn't listen. My imagination was in overdrive – we'd move to a smaller house; maybe I'd find a new man.

I had this strange notion that life would magically get back on track after our trip to Chicago.

A friend told me not to make plans but live in the moment. I found having nothing to look forward to in the future just brought me down. Grief was making me spiral and at six months in, I didn't know where I was. I didn't understand all these feelings of loss and guilt and anger and even some relief.

Sometimes I wonder if we ever understand what's going on.

Life Lessons

GROWING PAINS

While sorting out some old photos, Mum found an old black and white one of me chasing the boy next door. It is very cute; I was only about eighteen months old, but I'd grabbed hold and wasn't letting him go. Life was so simple then.

My childhood appeared idyllic, or perhaps I just look back with rose-tinted glasses. I enjoyed school because learning came easy but with hindsight, I'm not sure it was always so blissful.

There were difficult days. I took it badly when I didn't understand things; I hated being wrong. I remember playing on my own for much of the time, lost in my own imagination, although I did have friends and remember desperately trying to fit in.

Perhaps what I really loved was the structure of education and the long school holidays.

WHAT'S IN A NAME?

Scarffy was the family nickname passed from my uncles to my dad, then given to my older cousins before it became mine too. In my teens it was changed to Sexy Scarffy. A compliment, I first thought, rejoicing in the attention of the boys in my class. I wanted to be noticed by them. I would help them with their maths homework just for that spark of male attention. Until one boy called me 'tree trunk legs' as I walked home from school. From then on, I covered up, aware I was not really 'sexy', or worthy of being noticed.

TEENAGE CRUSHES

One Saturday afternoon I cycled to a boy's house and hand-delivered his not-so-secret Valentine's card. I was the sort of girl who liked to subvert convention even then.

His mum saw me at church the next day. 'He's not avoiding you; he's got Scouts.'

I bet he was glad of such a ready-made excuse.

I 'fancied' him on and off for years. That's the way my crushes went; none of them were ever reciprocated and when I finally got the chance of a first kiss from another boy, I ran away.

I felt odd until Andrew came along.

THE WRONG SHOES

They were the wrong type of shoes for a fourteen-year-old girl to wear. I thought they were stylish in the shop, more grown up than the usual school shoe selection.

On the carpet at home, they felt right, the heel making almost square indentations. In the mirror I looked taller, with just enough height to get noticed in the crowd.

I was seen, but in the way that makes you feel belittled and odd. After the laugher and teasing, I dramatically threw the offending footwear across the room, but sheepishly had to retrieve them.

I had nothing else to wear.

FRIENDSHIPS FORGED
IN THE SIXTH FORM COMMON ROOM

We felt the weight of disapproving glances aimed at us from the coffee bar, where the trendy students hung out.

What made us odd? Was it our clothes? Our shoes? Our accents? Our unashamed laughter at foolish things? The secret codes and quirky languages we devised?

Never invited to the cool parties, we organised our own 'social gatherings'. We had barbecues in the rain, contemplated life while sitting under a tree, wore nightshirts during the day for National Nightshirt week and made a joke telephone call that kept us in hysterics for weeks.

We are still friends to this day.

GAP YEAR

At the age of eighteen I deferred my place at polytechnic and took a gap year, which was not so common at the time. My aunt and uncle had emigrated to New Zealand when I was five and my mum promised I could stay with them for a year if I did well in my A levels. I didn't do that well, but at least I passed and the tickets were booked.

I'm not sure if my aunt and uncle ever had a say in this plan; they didn't have children, but instead had two pedigree Old English Sheepdogs. I didn't even like dogs and wondered briefly how I would survive, but excitement took over.

It was my first-ever flight and I flew to the other side of the world. Looking back, it is incredible to think I even did that, including a solo stopover in Los Angeles, visiting Disneyland and Universal Studios. According to my mum, Dad hardly slept until he knew I was safe and sound in New Zealand; this was years before mobile phones.

However, I don't think I took advantage of all that was on offer. I was still too young and naïve, with so much still to learn.

PEN PAL DISAPPOINTMENT

His handwriting was familiar; we'd written long chatty letters to each other all through our teens, even sent a few cassette tapes so I knew exactly how he sounded. I'd seen photos of him, where he lived, his pet rabbit, imaginatively called Rabbit. I wondered if he would be 'the one'? Our first meeting at the airport was stilted but we were chaperoned by my aunt and uncle, my surrogate parents for the year. We met again at the university when he was between lectures, I thought he was immature for a student. Maybe not really my type after all.

WILL I ALWAYS BE ODD?

My parents left school with no qualifications, and Dad especially couldn't understand why I wanted to carry on my education all the way to university.

In the end my grades were only good enough for a polytechnic, but a degree is a degree, whatever that really meant – I had no clue.

On my first day I wore a smart skirt, blouse and high heels; trying to make the best impression as a grown-up in the world of academia. Everyone else dressed down in jeans, relaxed and comfortable.

I had so much to learn, so many insecurities to shake off.

MEDIA STUDIES PROJECT: ENDANGERED ANIMALS

We giggled like schoolgirls while tucking our long hair inside our coats.

'Take your earrings off too,' the zookeeper said.

We never imagined they would let second-year students inside the cage to film. I always volunteered to be in front of the camera, while my friend was happy to take charge of the expensive equipment. We climbed in, oblivious to the animal scent by this stage, and sat down on the prickly straw. I'm sure most of the interview was squeals of delight as I tried to string together a coherent sentence with tiny gorilla fingers exploring my face.

STUDENT NIGHT

I twirled as best I could on the sticky nightclub floor to my favourite song. It was an elaborate display; years of dance classes had taught me how to spot and spin without getting dizzy; it was Malibu and coke that left me lightheaded. The Hungry Years near Brighton Pier wasn't the trendiest establishment but Thursday night was student night and it was the only place we ever frequented. As we went up the stairs to get in, we passed pictures of men queuing for food in the depression. Our hunger was for late eighties' dance tunes and cheap drinks.

GRADUATION CELEBRATION

There was a new doughnut shop in town. I chose one that was cream-filled with icing and sprinkles, sticky and sweet. I wore a mint green silk blouse and homemade waistcoat with pink roses on it. I'd made a special effort – it was graduation day. No summer ceremony for us. It was mid-winter in the middle of a snow storm so my parents couldn't make it, but I'd caught up with my friends so it wasn't a total waste. Then I heard Madonna on the radio, my mood lifted and somehow eating a doughnut on my own seemed celebration enough.

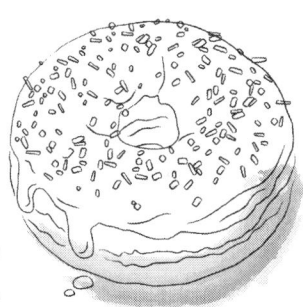

TIME TO GET A PROPER JOB

The deal I struck with Dad was I got a proper job. Having a degree in my pocket, even a 2:2, meant that should have been possible, but I was still ill-prepared for the real world, for any career that wasn't serving in a shop. My limited experiences and education didn't match up. I found my escape taking another gap year, along with some teenagers, volunteering in a church far away – in Yorkshire. I made new friends, embraced new challenges. I never found that elusive proper job, but I finally found the love and acceptance I'd always been searching for.

True Love

FIRST-EVER KISS AT TWENTY-THREE

He said I was nothing special, just the same as everybody else. I hated that; I wanted to be unique. I needed an explanation for my otherness, a reason why I felt so overlooked. He kissed me because I'd never been kissed before. He was doing me a favour or chalking me up as another conquest; I was the older woman.

Years later I compared notes with a friend; he had kissed her too at a party and by all accounts he was a well-practised and proficient kisser.

My lips now felt tainted.

And he said I was nothing special.

A SMALL BUT SIGNIFICANT DETOUR
ON THE ROAD TO TRUE LOVE

'Is this story about Dad?' asks my oldest son as he reads my words.

'No.'

'It's not clear.'

He's being honest. I value that and wonder if this belongs in my story at all.

It does because it is about words that are said which make you feel worthless, but also a first-ever kiss that should make your heart soar. Isn't this at the heart of all the fairy tales ever told?

I'd waited so long for this defining moment but when it was over I was left bitter, confused, and heartbroken. It was my crash course in young romance, but true love was not far away.

ANDREW

The first time I met Andrew was in a church hall for the youth group's Shorts and Shades disco. I never spoke to him that evening and I have no idea if he noticed me. He was too busy being the DJ. He wore jeans and a T-shirt and had straggly, unkempt hair, slightly sweaty with the excitement of putting on a show.

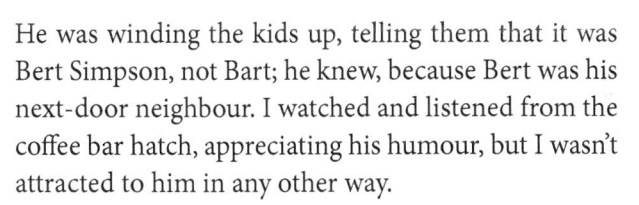

He was winding the kids up, telling them that it was Bert Simpson, not Bart; he knew, because Bert was his next-door neighbour. I watched and listened from the coffee bar hatch, appreciating his humour, but I wasn't attracted to him in any other way.

Our paths crossed, but not in a significant way until we started working on a radio project called Radio Cracker a year later.

MEETING BOB

'Come and see my dad,' he said.

We were in the hospital radio studio, a small room next to the chapel. We'd been recording jingles for a radio project. Andrew's voice was still DJ buoyant. 'He likes to see new people.'

I was intrigued, and my bewilderment grew as he led me out of the main building to one next door.

I expected to see a man like my dad, sitting up in bed in pyjamas with a cheery smile despite the pain. Instead, I saw an old man with the life knocked out of him.

This was the psychiatric unit and I was out of my comfort zone, but I put on a smile and followed Andrew's lead.

THE 'NO STRINGS' NOTE

A piece of paper rested on the mixing desk, folded over with my name on it. Andrew still loitered by the door, waiting for my response. The note was obviously from him, but I didn't recognise his handwriting at the time: very rounded, not joined up, almost childlike.

'Would you like to go out for a meal? No strings.'

Later that evening I dithered about throwing the note away. My hand hovered over the bin. I dropped the piece of paper and rescued it more than once, eventually deciding the note was not worth keeping but a 'date' might be fun.

SECOND DATE

Taking my hand, he helped me reach the summit of Roseberry Topping. We could see for miles. Tiny cars, unaware of us, travelled ribbon roads. We were alone. I wrapped my scarf tighter to keep out the December chill.

'I had a dream about you,' he said.

How should I reply to that?

Both of us were late developers where romance was concerned, inexperienced and unsure of the correct things to say on a second date. I felt the heat rising to my face as I blushed. I unwound the scarf again and stared out into the distance.

I wondered, where was that blue car heading? Anything to stop me wondering about this man and where this would lead.

PROBLEM SOLVER

My friend needed an ally to celebrate with, and I had nowhere else to be. Most guests were her boyfriend's single friends, who enjoyed playing games of Dungeons and Dragons.

New Year's Eve is the most elaborate game of all; it is supposed to be fun, alcohol-fuelled, ending with a kiss at midnight.

On a random roll of the dice, my new CD got stuck in someone else's new CD player.

'Andrew would take the machine apart!' I declared, certain that this name I had scattered like confetti all evening belonged to the man who could solve so many problems.

FROM A HOUSE TO A HOME

Sometime in 1990 Andrew bought a plot of land. I missed the construction phase and by the time I first visited in December 1992 there stood a split-level, upside-down house with magnolia walls throughout.

The brand-new kitchen appliances were barely used. There were oven chips and toffee ice cream in the freezer, a bottle of milk in the fridge and teabags beside the kettle.

We'd only just started dating but suddenly I was involved in choosing furniture and a picture for the bare walls.

On our first visit to IKEA together, a rite of passage into the adult world of homemaking, we came out with a lasagne dish.

'I like the idea of you cooking something in my kitchen,' he said.

The dish is chipped now, but I won't throw it out, even if I never make lasagne for one.

SO, WE ARE ENGAGED!

I always knew Andrew's proposal would never be romantic; it hung open-ended on untied strings between us. 'If we are still together at Christmas…' we said. By summer's end, we wondered why we were waiting.

'You don't have a ring!' My colleague was confused. She had been planning her engagement party for months. My blasé announcement upstaged her.

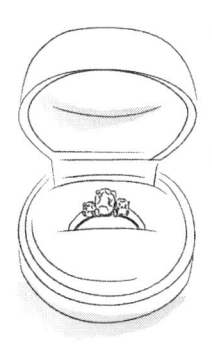

'We just decided to get married, so we are engaged!' The ring didn't matter, although we walked 'millions of miles' to find the right one, then had it customised to my own specifications when nothing in the case matched my ideal.

HE CALLED ME SALLY

It was a Sunday afternoon and you had collected your dad from the hospital to have Sunday lunch with us.

Your mum had gone to put the kettle on, and perhaps you had taken the dog around the block; anyway, suddenly I was alone with your dad.

He called me Sally and it startled me.

It only ever happened once and even in his locked-up world he appeared to immediately realise his mistake. I could see it deep in his eyes, a tacit understanding, a heartfelt apology that softened my shocked expression into a forgiving smile.

How I wish I'd known him when he was well and vibrant, before the heart attacks and strokes had crushed this large and gentle man. He now spent his days slumped in a chair, seemingly vacant, but he knew deep down his future daughter-in-law was not called Sally.

She was your ex-fiancé from years ago, best forgotten.

THE DAY YOUR DAD DIED

Every day you were offshore you rang me, always greeting me the same way.

'Hello you, any news?'

I had to think of something exciting to report about life at home. At best a snippet of gossip to share, often a dull comment on the weather.

Today was different. I'd already spoken to your mam, and I had to break the news to you that your dad had died in the night.

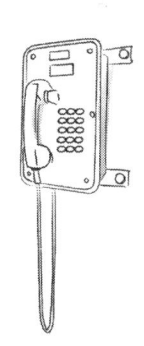

I'd never passed on bad news like this before, even face to face. How did I find the right words to both break your heart and soothe it?

From This Day Forward

WEDDING PLANS

We married in the Baptist church where I had been a volunteer because this was where we met, and our original thinking was that Andrew's dad would be able to join us. We had time to change the venue after he died, but it still made sense to celebrate our wedding where our love had grown.

Our wedding wasn't exactly 'done on the cheap', but we were both practical and neither of us wanted to waste money on fripperies.

Andrew loved the fact I was low maintenance. After years of working offshore he always stated, 'No grabby woman is getting her hands on my money.'

To show off my frugality and other talents, I made my dress; the fabric only cost me £100. As the day got closer, I started to worry I hadn't spent enough on fabric and trimmings. We borrowed Andrew's brother's two-seater car to drive away in rather than hire something fancy; who needs a chauffeur?

My flowers were silk rather than real and I can't think why now, except I wanted blue flowers in my bouquet. Blue roses don't exist and I thought real flowers that had been dyed blue looked tacky. It did mean my bouquet lasted far longer than my marriage, although eventually they got too dusty, slightly dishevelled and I binned them.

RUNAWAY BRIDE?

There's a video clip somewhere of me running away from the church on our wedding day. I wasn't having second thoughts, I arrived bang on time, so worried you wouldn't wait for me. You told me not to be late and at the grand old age of twenty-six I thought this day would never come. I tugged at my dad's hand, leading him across the road to the church. But you were still outside, having photos taken with your brothers, at thirty-two you were the last to get married, perhaps the least likely. Somehow, we had found each other and this was what I always wanted.

TRADITION

'You have to carry my over the threshold, it's tradition.'

'Don't be silly.'

I stood resolute, unmoving in my white, homemade dress.

'Come in. The others will be here soon with the presents.'

'I'm not coming in until you carry me.'

'But I might drop you.'

I stared at him, suddenly worried he might drop me on purpose.

I found out through the years that marriages are made of battles lost and won, compromises struck.

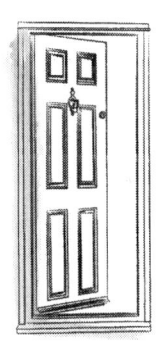

'Just over the threshold,' I pleaded, almost ready to give in, when he lifted me up, setting me down in the hallway as I requested.

THE SECRET CODE OF HOLDING HANDS

You said we would always hold hands, even when we were old and grey. I wonder if it was appropriate to hold hands through a church service? Hands clasped out of sight, hidden between dark wooden pews that probably held many secrets. You took my hand in yours and traced the words 'I love you' on my palm. I squeezed your hand tight in a warning, catching the glint in your eye that threatened an eruption of laughter. We communicated simply, secretly, lovingly. Now I can only remember as I bring a hand to my face to trace a tear.

HONEYMOON AROUND THE WORLD

I remember driving to see earthquake-cracked roads, I remember a tour up into the mountains on a rickety truck with a guide called William, I remember a harbour cruise on a boat that wasn't plush and extravagant but your smile shone brighter than moonlight.

I can't remember you getting hassled by queues, or bothered when I was stopped at security for packing my earrings in a tin which showed up as something suspicious on the X-ray machine. We laughed it off.

What broke you and let the depression in?

Keeping our passports, once used and stamped, left in the drawer.

STILL SPINNING

Your vast record collection held the memories of my youth. Dancing in the kitchen with my dad, crushes on boys who never noticed me at youth club, meaningful lyrics that I copied into notebooks. Every disc was catalogued and labelled, held together in a green ring binder.

'Play this one,' I said. 'Don't Leave Me This Way', by The Communards, number 777 in your collection.

You were a great DJ, but it was years after you died that I discovered the trophy you won for your efforts. It was two days after you died that I discovered the turntable in the den was still spinning.

LIFE AS A GROWN-UP

You jumped as I caught you unawares, headphones on, lost in your own world. Were you pretending you were the star? I really believed you could be if you had the lucky break you deserved.

Did you believe as much in me?

'I want to write. Can I sign up for this course? Look, you can earn your money back.'

My words tumbled out too quickly. Once again, I'd caught you unawares, but this time I was the more startled.

'It's a con,' you said, squashing my dreams with just a few words when I needed your support.

Years later you bought me a laptop. 'Of course I believe in you, but you don't know the right people to be published.'

For far too long I believed you and boxed up my glittery childhood dreams of doing anything creative.

It was time to be a grown-up, a wife and maybe soon a mother.

THIRD ARM

'What would you do with a third arm?'

We never came up with any useful conclusions, just ended up going round in circles each Tuesday evening in the pub, just before last orders.

Andrew seemed the odd one of the group, a pint of coke before him instead of beer. Invited by his brother, he went along when he wasn't offshore.

I joked he had no friends of his own, then I tagged along after him, another spare part. They were all invited to our wedding, and Tuesday evenings continued as before. Until we had children, then everything changed.

For Better

FAMILY MULTIPLICATION

If getting married changes a lot of things in life, having children changes everything. It was the next logical step and fortunately we conceived easily the first time around.

Our family grew and I found a new purpose in being a mum. There was no time for my daydreams where I was the star of the show.

I'd long ago given up the idea of being a dancer, maybe I could still do something on the stage, or make up stories and write, one day, sometime in the future. For now, my energy was focused on this tiny new person I had helped create.

CHRISTMAS BABY NUMBER ONE

I find the photo of you as a new dad looking terrified by responsibility, as I suppose all new dads do.

I'm twenty-eight but look barely eighteen, Madonna-like with flowing auburn hair.

Our son was late and heavy; maybe I am still high on the gas and air I was given earlier when they stitched me up, while you sat there cradling our boy.

From here I only remember the good bits, writing Christmas cards with an extra name, seeing our new-born blinking under twinkling tree lights, you being home for the holidays. Everything sprinkled with festive glitter.

NEW MUMS

Our first meeting was in a room at the local cottage hospital, talking about birth plans and what to expect, although nothing really prepared us. Months later we pushed our shiny prams along the streets together and arranged weekly meet-ups at each other's houses.

When our babies could all sit upright, we arranged them in a line on the sofa and took photos. We compared notes about feeding, sleeping patterns and sore nipples; few topics were off limits. Mine was the youngest, shuffling on his bottom rather than crawling, the last to learn to walk.

We were all learning.

MOTHER'S DAY

'No one told me it would be so hard.' I was crying on my mum's shoulder; she had arrived earlier on the train on this special day. Every time Andrew left for work, I had to be a single mum for the next two weeks. Holding everything together on my own was tough. Mum stroked my hair and calmed my fears. Her parents had been a short bus ride away when we were tiny; today's journey had taken her half a day by train. Geography and circumstances pulled us in opposite directions, but this thing called motherhood held us together fast.

UNFORGETTABLE NIGHTSHIFT

We'd had a restless night, I have no idea why, couldn't tell you how many times I'd been up in the night, but finally I'd settled my son in the bed beside me, a special treat we sometimes enjoyed when his dad was away.

It was still quite early when the phone rang, but Andrew was on nights so it wasn't unexpected.

'Hello,' I whispered over the head of our sleeping child.

'Princess Diana's died,' he said, quite matter-of-factly. 'We've been watching the news unfold all night.'

In the middle of the North Sea, he had lived through every minute of this 'where were you when' moment. The unexpected early death of a woman born in 1961, the same year as him.

Maybe this made him question his own mortality?

Meanwhile I thought of her two young sons thrust into the limelight to grieve the loss of a parent and drew my sleeping son closer.

CHRISTMAS BABY NUMBER TWO

We never intended to have two December birthdays; it seemed not much was going to plan when we discovered the baby was breech.

Manipulation by the consultant wasn't successful so they decided to allay my fears of having a C-section by inviting me to look round the delivery room, dispel the mystique.

I wasn't reassured. I'd never had an operation before, except having my wisdom teeth out, and I couldn't see those scars.

Terrified, I prayed harder than ever before, asking God for a much-needed miracle as I lay on my bed with my bum in the air. Not very holy I will admit, but I was desperate.

I thought I felt something but almost dared not to believe it until they examined me. They wheeled in the portable ultrasound, and the clinician, who usually wore the most perfect poker face, broke into a rare smile.

The baby's head was down; they gave me tea and toast and sent me home.

One week later, our second son was delivered naturally by the same midwife as his older brother. I'd always thought I wanted a girl, but I couldn't have been more delighted.

LIMPET

Youngest son never suffered the terrible twos; instead, he was adorable, if a touch clingy. Oldest son was five, with testosterone surging through his little body, school friends shaping his thoughts and actions in new ways. Mum rang. 'I've been diagnosed with breast cancer. I need a mastectomy.' I lived so far away; I didn't know what I could do from here. I was beginning to spiral downwards.

Should I go to the doctor? Andrew beat me to it; he got the little white pills a long time before I did. I became the family rock, strengthened by my limpet.

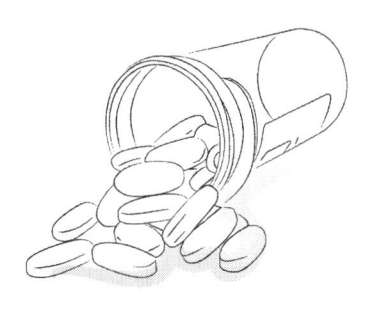

DREAM HOME

My walk to the baby clinic took me past the grandest house in the village. I peeked in at the expansive garden, a playground with a swing, a treehouse and so much room to run. Our family was only small, but this would be the perfect place for us to grow. It was no more than a fleeting dream, and I'd almost forgotten it until we found it for sale in the property pages. We were a family of four now, six if you included the guinea pigs.

'Shall we take a look?' you asked.

I nodded as the dream reawakened.

UNEXPECTED DETOURS MAKE THE BEST DAYS OUT

We saw signs for a sheepdog trial. 'Innocent or guilty?' You joked. Curiosity got the better of us and we could have sat on that Welsh hillside all day, making up our own commentary, but the boys were soon restless. How old were they then? Seven and four or six and three? I should remember each holiday more clearly, let's be honest they were few and far between.

Unexpected detour days were always the best. Remember following the signs to the National Space Centre, on a whim, so out of character, we drove for miles but it was worth it.

BEDTIME

"Did you shut the gate?"

"Yes."

"Lock the front door?'"

'Of course.'

I'd already be in bed reading, cosy and snug, glad to have Andrew home to take care of things.

Naturally, I could do it all myself; half the time I had to, but it is comforting to be looked after.

'Your feet are cold!' I'd cry out as he slipped into bed beside me.

I'd put my book down, making compromises; he preferred I didn't keep the light on and read for long. We would cuddle, discuss the day, then turn our backs on each other and sleep.

PEACOCK

'Sarah, come quickly, there's a peacock in the garden.'

I searched for a display of bright-coloured plumage, but all I could see was a common pheasant.

Andrew had been brought up on industrial Teesside and I was a country girl, but did he really not know the difference?

I never let him forget his mistake; isn't that how marriage works? Keeping account of funny anecdotes to share... At least, I found it funny, but I hated it when he reminded me of my own lack of knowledge.

We all want to strut proudly and not be made the fool.

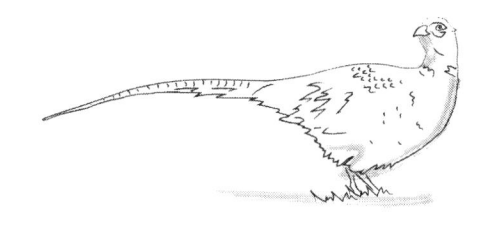

For Worse

DEPRESSION

With spending so much time away from home working, Andrew was always reticent to go anywhere on holiday. Being home for him was a treat. That made holidays difficult at the best of times; on more than one occasion we came home earlier than expected. It was always me who had to hand the keys back and explain a 'change of plan'.

'I knew you wouldn't stay the whole week,' said one man with great insight, as he took the keys from me. Perhaps this happens more times than we realise.

When Andrew's depression got especially bad, it wasn't just holidays that suffered. I arranged family days out for three instead of four, kept the children quiet and amused. I felt I was walking on eggshells and often found myself diminishing, rarely getting what I really wanted, often feeling resentful, sometimes wishing Andrew wasn't here at all.

This was when we first visited Chicago.

WISH YOU WERE HERE

I accepted the invitation to fly away, and holiday with friends – without you.

Much went unsaid as I packed suitcases for three, not four. Was this the make-or-break precipice of our marriage?

The boys enjoyed our adventure. We saw the sights, rode in a speedboat at twilight, ate real Chicago pizza, saw a shooting star over the drive-in movie screen. I wished all the time you were there with us.

In a gift shop I found a small smooth stone that nestled in the palm of my hand. Gold letters spelled out the word SOULMATE. The perfect holiday present for you.

DEEP DEPRESSION

It was Saturday afternoon and I was outside Woolworths when you rang. As I pressed the phone close to my ear to listen, I could hear your tears, as salty as the sea which separated us. Depression had sunk its teeth in deep, and you couldn't cope with work. You would be on the flight home tomorrow. I tried to reassure you, hoping my words were the right ones, trying to be the strong one. Busy shoppers hurried past with no notion of how my world was shifting as I stood firm, offering up a silent prayer for your safe return.

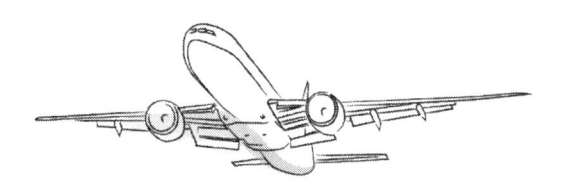

A SPECIAL DAY OUT

We gave up on conventional holidays and made a new plan, to each choose a day out in the summer. Andrew chose High Force Waterfall; we waited for the perfect day. It started with a phone call from Mum telling me my uncle had died. Suddenly there was no time to waste; life is a fragile thing to be enjoyed. We woke the boys; I made sandwiches and we set off. They skimmed stones after our picnic, we laughed, then stopped some tourists to take a photo of the four of us – the very last photo taken of our family.

ORDINARY SATURDAY MAGIC

Andrew's mam made proper chips on Saturdays. There were plump sausages and crispy bacon too. A fried egg for Andrew, a delicacy, as I don't eat eggs so never cooked one for him. The boys stayed over on a Friday evening; watching quiz shows and playing dominoes with Grandma was a treat for them and a night off for us.

That Saturday was no different except when we arrived home, we spied a whole family of pheasants running across the lawn, their skinny legs moving quickly, rounded bodies bobbing. We sat in the car in wonder, watching this happy family.

EXPECT THE UNEXPECTED

'Please let me read it to you.'

Just a few hundred words, written for the local community magazine. We were between vicars, and those on the leadership team were taking it in turns to write something for our church page. It was almost Christmas so I'd written about the surprising nature of the Nativity.

'Expect the Unexpected.'

Andrew listened to my written words for probably the first time ever.

'Very Radio 4,' was his assessment, but he had listened. I never kept a printed copy; I was too caught up in my own unexpected drama. Suddenly my words sounded trite.

THERE WAS A RAINBOW

I sang a worship song in the car that day, praising God whose love endures forever.

Andrew was feeling much better, more hopeful. A few days before, he drew me in close and kissed me in front of a friend, watching us from our kitchen table, without his usual embarrassment.

The familiar road towards the sea twisted and turned. I passed the flowers left for a fatality earlier in the year, a young family man, so sad, but then I saw the rainbow full of promise in the sky, getting brighter as I sang louder.

Two days later, Andrew died.

Till Death Do Us Part

WHAT IS THIS THING CALLED GRIEF?

At the beginning of 2010 things had been getting back on track. Counselling, tablets, and a change of circumstance at work all contributed to Andrew's improved mood.

'The old Andrew is coming back,' he told me more than once. I knew the road ahead wouldn't be easy, but perhaps we had turned a corner.

About a week before he died, I woke in the night and discovered Andrew wasn't in bed beside me. I found him on the landing, crouched over in the same face down, foetal position I found him in when he had his fatal heart attack. I wonder now if it was a foreshadowing of what was to come.

On that occasion I just talked him back to bed, believing there was nothing really wrong; it was just a tiny blip in the road, barely noticed. I'm not sure Andrew even believed me when I told him about it the next morning.

But here I was six months after Andrew died, with friends, somewhere outside Chicago, in tears, ringing my parents, asking them to take the boys for the rest of the school holiday while I tried to sort my life out. In true Nicholson style, we were cutting our holiday short. I wondered if I'd ever manage a full holiday ever again.

I had only just begun to scratch the surface of understanding what grief was all about.

I started on antidepressants and had some counselling, although it took three attempts to find a counsellor who really helped me.

As we reached the end of the school summer term, the end of primary school for youngest son, we had an important task to complete – scattering Andrew's ashes.

Like most things, I had it all planned out. I'd written my story; I knew exactly how and where we would say goodbye – but it didn't happen that way. Scattering the ashes took two attempts.

INTENTIONS

'If I wanted to end it, I'd run off the cliff.' I struggled to comprehend you ever entertained such thoughts in your head. It was a dramatic and visceral way to go.

An unbidden memory dropped in my head of an argument we'd once had, ending with me hiding car keys in the toe of a wellington boot by the front door. I wanted to stop you driving away in anger. A tangled car crash could have such far reaching consequences.

Now I realise what a useless act it was; we had always lived within walking distance from the clifftop.

PLANS IN THE WIND

It was a summer afternoon when we set off full of purpose. In my rucksack was a cardboard container, the colour of a Christmas tree, the size of a shoebox, the weight of a new-born baby.

I told the boys, 'We will scatter Dad's ashes over the cliff, walk along into town, have fish and chips for tea and get the bus back.'

I had it all figured out, until the first handful black ash blew back in our faces. You had no intentions of leaving us here.

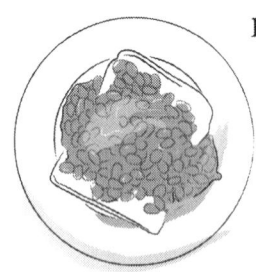

Defeated, we marched back home and had beans on toast for tea.

PLAN B – FINALLY FREE

As we drove away from the coast to higher ground, a mist rolled over the heather, creating the sort of spooky atmosphere you loved. I wasn't sure if I knew the way. Narrow roads twisted and turned, and we kept climbing until miraculously we reached the right spot. I probably said a few words, but they were carried away on the breeze along with your ashes which flew so freely, swirling as if you had found your forever home. Out in the wilderness, the middle of nowhere. You were truly happy here, and we could leave you safe and sound.

A BOX OF MATCHES

Your heavy-duty coat rattles as I lift if off the hook. Loose matches have escaped the box like explosive pick-up sticks.

This was the coat you wore while lighting the fireworks for us and our friends. Our expansive garden used to its full potential, plenty of safe space from disaster. The kids sat on the climbing frame to watch, while the adults cradled mugs of soup in cold hands.

The Catherine wheel didn't spin and left a scorch mark on the tree. Irrevocably scarred.

I count the matches back into the box and fold the coat to give away.

MESSAGE IN A BOTTLE

The support acts were nothing special, but we were down on the pitch soaking up the atmosphere, waiting for the headline act. Beer bottles were flying high in the air. I watched them, wondering what would happen if someone got hit.

Considering I was looking up, I still didn't see it coming right for my eye. Oldest son took me to first aid; they assessed me and handed me some paracetamol, but otherwise didn't seem too concerned.

It was only later as we watched from the stands that I realised my tears were caused more by raw grief than pain.

RECYCLED

'You're murdering Dad's sweatshirt!' youngest son cried.

'No, I'm recycling it,' I replied, brandishing the needlework scissors.

For a man who loved anything plain to wear, Andrew did have a thing for patterned sweatshirts, and this was without doubt his favourite. He wore it on special days, I have photos to prove it - the first day of the new millennium and three years earlier, when our eldest son was born. The soft fabric was worn, but still strong enough to make a new bag.

I laid it out flat on the table and prepared to make the first cut.

WOODCHIP ON THE CEILING

In the mood for mischief and mayhem, I bounced on the bed, my fingers reaching for the edge of the loose wallpaper. It was already coming unstuck, as so much in our old house was. Whoever thought woodchip on the ceiling was a good idea? I bounced and plucked; thin strips free-falling. Then I hit the jackpot as almost a whole sheet rippled down on top of me. I lay there giggling, staring up at the complete mess I had made.

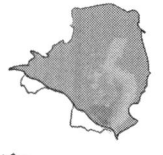

For a moment I wondered what you would have said.

Then I laughed louder without a care.

A MODERN-DAY PARABLE OF THE WIDOW IN THE SHOWER

The campsite shower block was typically damp and bleak. Arriving towel in hand, I found one cubicle free and one lady waiting.

'That one's not great,' she said. 'Just a dribble. I'm waiting for another.'

'It doesn't bother me,' I replied, with the bravado of someone who has given up expecting good things to happen.

However, as the inevitable trickle miraculously burst into a perfect cascade, I had a sense of God pouring blessings down on me. I'd freely accepted less than the best and was given so much more.

At this Christian conference I was living my own modern-day parable.

BORROWED JUMPERS

You never wore the hand-knitted Aran sweater I found squashed in the back of the wardrobe. Perhaps it was too tight for you, but it fitted my pre-baby body perfectly.

'Sally made that.' Seeing my face fall, you added, 'Well, she started it, but Mam did most of it.'

You said you didn't mind if I wore it, but I made it disappear soon after.

Now you are gone, I wear your favourite baggy blue jumper on the coldest days, the lonely days, the can't be bothered to do anything, just want to hide days.

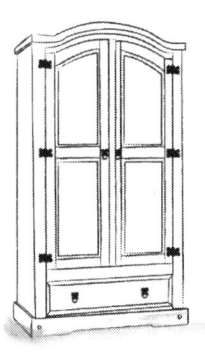

I hope you don't mind.

IN THE WAITING ROOM

The Carpenters' greatest hits should have been the perfect soothing soundtrack for a doctors' waiting room. I remembered an afternoon long ago, just me and Andrew listening to Karen Carpenter sing loudly from the next-door neighbour's open window. We never complained. Many of their songs would have gone down a treat while I flicked through the out-of-date, obscure magazines, but today I was treated to the mournful lyrics about lost love and heartache. Hardly appropriate listening for a grieving widow collecting her monthly prescription for antidepressants. Buoyed with happy memories I see the funny side; the tablets are obviously working.

HARSH WORDS

I'm tucking youngest son into bed, conscious there are still things I need to do this evening, but he does that trick where he grabs my hand and won't let go.

'Grandma and Grandad are coming tomorrow,' I say.

'Why do the bossy people have to come and stay?'

He prefers my lax and flexible routines; these days I am a pushover who gives in easily.

'I need my mum and dad around to help sometimes.'

'I don't have a dad anymore.'

His words are harsh and they sting.

And I have no words to say back to him, so I just hold on a little longer, a little tighter.

Survival

WE SURVIVED THE FIRST YEAR!

We had a party in November 2011, a fiftieth birthday party for Andrew, although he wasn't there.

At the funeral it had all been so easy to stand up and talk about him, my words prepared in black and white in front of me, but at the party when I spoke, unscripted and from the heart, I fell apart, got tongue-tied and ended up feeling wretched.

I wish I'd have said how wonderful Andrew was, a good provider and a great father. I should have mentioned how much he made me smile, how safe I felt in his arms. I wanted to say how much I missed him and tell of that special relationship we shared.

The truth was it was often easier to remember the tough times, the difficulties we faced, because then I could be glad Andrew was no longer around.

However, as I looked at all my friends that evening, each one married, I wanted to remind them how lucky they were. How their partner was worth holding onto, despite the daily disagreements and disappointments of married life. How often I yearn for someone special to hold my hand. How much I wish I had someone to reveal my deepest thoughts to. How lonely it is when the whole is ripped apart.

The truth is they know how I feel and are aware of what they've got.

We had survived the first year as a family of three; now we had to put the broken pieces back together and learn to live with the aftermath in all the years that followed.

SCARS

'You'll have a great scar,' I told him. 'When you get a girlfriend, she'll love it!' He looked at me with the typical distain of a teenage boy to his mother, as if I was mad.

'I'd rather not have a scar at all.'

Wouldn't we all! No scars, no bruises, no visible marks to show the life we have lived.

Running into a tennis net post was not in his plans today. Becoming a widow at forty-two was not my ambition either.

Both events came out of the blue and took time to recover from, but scars fade in time.

A RUDE AWAKENING

It would have been our nineteenth or maybe twentieth wedding anniversary when the kitchen ceiling fell down. It was also four o'clock in the morning.

I jumped out of bed and ran downstairs to see what all the commotion was. I switched on the light and, unfazed by the mess, resolved to clear it up at a more sensible hour.

The hot-water tank had been leaking for a while. I'd watched the brown stain travelling slowly out of the corner of my eye. I'd got used to the household disasters and my list of useful phone numbers was growing.

LIVING WITH BROKEN THINGS

'Mum, I think I've broken the fridge!' My son, I can't remember which, was so apologetic in his confession. I came to look and discovered it was only the handle that had come off.

'We can get a new one.'

'Fridge?' He looked dismayed, obviously worrying about the cost to fix his heavy-handedness.

'No, just a replacement handle.'

Or we could learn to live with it broken, like we learned to live without a dad in the house. The fridge still worked perfectly fine; you just prised the door open with your fingers.

We rarely gave it a second thought.

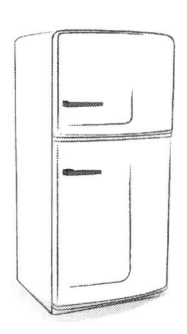

ON GOD'S PENDING PILE

Sometimes my faith is strong and certain, like the words that run through a stick of rock.

At other times it is as fragile as a fingernail, and I'm barely hanging on.

But most of the time I feel I am on God's pending pile; the answer always seems to be WAIT.

He dismisses me with a wan smile as if this is not my time; didn't I have a miracle back in '99 with baby number two?

How long must I wait? Do I get another one?

Weren't there promises in a shower? Imminent blessings on their way?

The years pass and my house still doesn't sell and my dreams don't come true.

And then my dad gets cancer.

And the house next door is falling down.

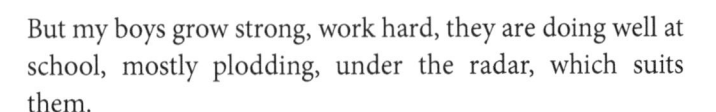

But my boys grow strong, work hard, they are doing well at school, mostly plodding, under the radar, which suits them.

But I want the glitter; I've trudged too long through treacle.

God, when will you answer me?

With a real answer that isn't just WAIT!?

MY MARY MOMENT

I finally get to play the Virgin Mary in a school Nativity at the age of forty-four.

Confident readers at school are most likely to be the narrator, with no chance to dress up or perform.

Now, with a team from church, I was acting out Bible stories in school assemblies each week. I flexed my dramatic muscles, so often taking on the bigger roles, and Mary is obviously essential.

She is also quiet, serene and compliant. Nothing like me.

I cradle the doll in my arms, acting out my silent contemplation. The children watch in awe, the team in amusement.

FRIDAY TEA

The Le Creuset pan on the Aga top is bubbling away and a large table takes centre stage in the impressive kitchen. The scene resembles a middle-class 1980s sitcom with preparations taking place for a cosy supper party, but the Muppet music plays on the radio as I dance around, excited to once again host Friday Tea.

This is a gathering of our church family each week to share pre-packed pizzas alongside home-cooked fare of risottos and chilli and cheesy-topped lasagne. This is followed by chocolate fingers, snaffled by youngest son and taken to the playroom, while the grown-ups delight in seasonal fruit crumble and homemade cake.

When we've had our fill, other people's husbands gather plates and do the washing up. I'll let anyone take over in my kitchen these days. Everyone knows how to boil the kettle on the Aga for a cuppa. This is family.

ONE OF THOSE DAYS

Rain again, big heavy drops of it bouncing on the roof – it was sunny an hour ago, but now the blue skies have been obliterated once more by dirty grey clouds.

It's been one of 'those' days.

A friend posted a gorgeous photo of a rainbow on his Facebook page. His office is high up, so the view of colour tumbling to the streets below was particularly striking.

No rainbows here – I've searched – it's hopeless.

It's been one of 'those' days.

Sunshine and showers.

Laughter and tears.

Tissues and chocolate required in equal measure.

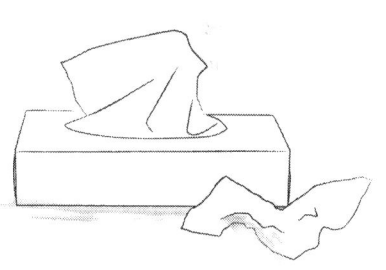

And now my free time is running out, being squeezed just as the words start to flow.

But I just needed to tell you…

It's been one of 'those' days.

GARDEN LEAVES

Our garden, a source of joy. Somewhere to play, to marvel at creation. On mild autumn days I would sweep the leaves, a thankless task as more were sure to fall overnight, and yet it stilled my soul, kept me in tune with nature; it also gave me a link back in time to the days when this was your job. Now most tasks are mine alone and some are resented. I've never got on top of all the paperwork inside. Out here, a swept lawn brings a satisfaction like no other, entwined with a deep sorrow at my loss.

HOMECOMING

There's a crunch of tyres on the gravel, a car door shutting, keys in the lock and the front door opening, with a familiar scratch of a small stone caught underneath scraping on the tiles.

My son is safely home and I am attuned to every noise he makes.

It's not that long ago that he passed his test. He drives the car that used to belong to Andrew.

The sound of his arrival also takes me back to a time when the homecoming would have been his dad, my husband, my beloved.

Sounds of another adult in the house that I've not heard for years both unsettle and soothe me.

FOR THE LOVE OF GREEN

'The house is too big' or 'it's not quite in the right location'.

What did people expect of a seven-bedroom property surrounded by ex-council houses?

The location that suited us was never going to be everyone's cup of tea. Occasionally the rejection was more interesting; one lady unbelievably said the kitchen was too small!

Another: 'There's a lot of green in the house and I don't like the colour green.' Luscious Lime, Overtly Olive, I could list all the alliterative paint colours on our walls.

Green featured in almost every room, just like bits of Lego and IKEA furniture.

HAPPY FIFTIETH

It bugs me looking back at photos that I had the wrong-coloured tights on; I should have thought about it and bought new ones, but I will be forever low maintenance, just the way Andrew liked me to be.

Everything else was pretty much perfect. My bright red nails matched my spotty red dress. Snowdrops from the garden adorned each table. I'd arranged the perfect caterers and I was surrounded by friends. The eighties' playlist got us on our feet.

I pushed aside thoughts that Andrew should have been here spinning the records; he never even made it to fifty.

LEAVING HOME

I was once used to the sight of bags in the hallway, part of the onshore, offshore rota. The bags today belong to youngest son, along with a box of food, rolled-up duvet, and a rucksack with the nose of a soft toy penguin peeking out from the pocket, which makes me smile. New adventures beckon for him and the beginning of the empty nesting process for me. Soon I will be packing away everything else in this home which is too big a house for one. I plan my own adventures, unaware of the next curve ball coming my way.

Everything Changes

THE BEST LAID PLANS

In eight years, our lives had changed dramatically. I felt ready for a new challenge. Oldest son had finished university, moved out and started his dream job, youngest son was just starting his degree. I had finally managed to sell the house that was once our dream home. I was preparing for a long-distance move back to sunny Suffolk.

So many friends said, 'That's such a long way to go.'

Then I remembered the only plan Andrew and I had for our future was when his mum died, we would move closer to my parents.

My mother-in-law had died a few years earlier, and now my dad was having chemotherapy, it made sense to be close by to help out now my parents needed me more.

I dreamed of building a new, exciting life; maybe without the boys to consider I could find some much longed-for romance in my life, or I could finally travel, generally put myself first and do the things I'd dreamed of. Perhaps even finish the memoir about grief that I longed to write.

A month or so before I was set to move, I started having hospital tests for some unexplained aches and pains. The results weren't good; just like my dad, I had cancer.

Then the beautiful new home by the sea that I'd set my heart on fell through. I would have to move out of my house, put my furniture in storage and move in with my parents temporarily.

I was set adrift, wondering, waiting and angry with God that he had allowed more heartache to be dumped at my door.

DIAGNOSED

I squashed a juicy cherry between the roof of my mouth and my tongue, enjoying the explosion of flavour. Cherry pie had always been my favourite. Who knew if I'd ever get to eat it again.

Only minutes ago, the consultant had said, 'What's more important, moving or your health?'

I was hysterical. This was a decision no one should have to make. The moving date was set for three weeks' time.

He thought I should be prepping for the op rather than packing.

'Moving is for my health,' I said decisively to my friend, taking another bite of delicious pie.

A QUESTION OF TIMING?

Did I make the right choice? I'm still here, aren't I?

How I put on a brave face and got organised I will never know.

The grace of God?

The help of friends?

The sheer bloody-minded determination?

I heard the house clearance men bag up and drag the heavy items from the den, trying not to think of all the happy times, sitting there with Andrew. So much stuff thrown away, discarded, I should be free at last, unburdened, but inside the cancer hadn't stopped growing, weighing me down with a new set of baggage for the next adventure.

AND THE WINNER IS...

The award ceremony was only an hour away from my parents', but Dad booked me a taxi so I didn't need to drive.

Fortunately, I felt well on that day, able to eat and keep down the delicious three-course meal and even drink champagne to celebrate.

My dress was borrowed from my mum, embellished with just the right amount of sparkle for the mother of a nominee.

No one knew what was growing inside me, how my insides churned; they just saw the outer glow of a proud mother delighting in her son's success, trainee sports journalist of the year.

EMERGENCY STOMA

'You may end up with a bag.'

I was well past caring. They could cut me open and do whatever they liked to stop the pain. Dying almost seemed a good option, but then the boys would be orphans; best not think about that.

I drifted off anaesthetised and awoke in Critical Care discombobulated and bruised.

There was the bag – my internal plumbing reconfigured. Inside the bag a stoma, a pink protrusion from my tummy. I still marvel at it. Sometimes a tight rosebud, nowhere near as fragrant, sometimes an alien moving of its own accord.

Always a life saver.

FIFTY-ONE YEARS YOUNG

It's my fifty-first birthday, not one you ordinarily make a fuss of, but this is special. I am alive and all the cancer had been removed. Yippee!

The oncologist recommends a 'belt and braces' approach as I am young; I guess it's all relative, so today I started chemo – coordinated so I have my appointment at the same time as my dad.

We sit across from one another for our family outing, several large chairs, drip stands and medical paraphernalia squeezed into the GP's room.

New friends made, new sensations, soft voices, regular beeping, and birthday cake to share.

THE UNWRITTEN RULES OF CHEMO

There is a lull between the beeping machines, leaving space for a catch-up. Dad regales us with news of his garden, someone doing the crossword calls out a clue, then I work out that the lady sitting opposite me today was in the cancer ward with me a few weeks ago. Another unexpected blip when my grumbly gall bladder had to be removed.

'Remember the young woman in with us, in the bed by the window?' I said softly. 'I found out she died last week.'

Dad glared at me. One of the nurses, visibly shaken, turns her head away. I'm sure she wiped away a tear.

'You never talk about death in there,' Dad scolded later as we left.

A HOME OF MY OWN

It is Easter time when I move from my parents' to my new home. I have been living with them since before Christmas. The boxes, so long in storage, arrive ready to be unpacked.

This is the start of a new chapter, but I'm sluggish from chemo and taking things easy, aware this is not quite the auspicious start I wanted. Or even the house of my dreams. This was all fields when I was young.

My new neighbour is seven years old; he says the man who used to live here was grumpy, so he's glad I've moved in instead. His mum tells him not to be so rude.

Later he drops round a homemade card and I smile as I stick it to my new fridge, with a fully working handle.

ENCOURAGEMENT

Chemo derailed us as a family and we need some adventures to make up for our lost summer. I book a treetop experience.

Oldest signs the waiver form without a second glance; he appears to listen to the safety briefing in the same indifferent manner. He's always so sure of anything physical and appears unaware of dangers.

Youngest is determined to read the paperwork word for word; he's conscientious to a fault.

I skim the standard text and leave my mark.

The first two climbs are fine but by the third I am getting fearful of the letting go, even when I know the harness is secure.

Suddenly I am in the moment, aware of peril, aware that only three weeks ago I was still regularly being pumped full of toxins. My body is still recovering.

'You can do this.' Youngest takes my hand, helps me step by step; suddenly our roles reversed as he cares for me with tenderness and understanding beyond his years.

I let the boys tackle the final climbs on their own, enjoying their laughter, looking up and marvelling at everything around me.

PERIPHERAL NEUROPATHY

I sit in the dentist's waiting room and marvel when the dental nurse runs up the flight of stairs.

'I used to be able to do that,' I think.

Part of me is mystified about when I lost this superpower, but I know full well it went hand in hand with a cancer diagnosis – or, more accurately, chemotherapy treatment.

Poison pumped through my body killing bad cells and good ones without differentiation. Nerve endings irreparably damaged. Every step a reminder; if I want it to be.

My name is called and I cross the room, only conscious of my smile.

NATURE LESSONS

'Let's go a different way home,' says Dad.

We turn off and stop at a village pond where he points out the fish making tiny ripples in the water.

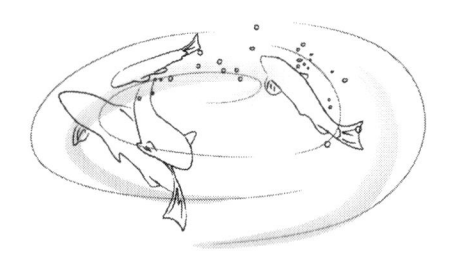

I remember a much grander lake, a stately home, a family holiday. Mum took a photo of me and Dad and my brother sitting on a log, Dad pointing in the distance, us looking out in wonder – all staged for the camera. There was nothing particular to see.

Today is different, a precious 'father and daughter' moment. I'm not pretending. I need to see everything he wants to show me.

WEDNESDAY WOBBLE

News of the pandemic is alarming and causing me to wobble. I didn't go to Pilates, but went for a solo walk instead to clear my head. Am I vulnerable? My chemo only finished six months ago. I don't want to feel so fragile. I worry about the boys, so far away. The university is suspending all face-to-face teaching and I need my 'little boy' home. The older one will have to fend for himself, but I hate all the unknowns.

I share my worries on Facebook for posterity.

A friend leaves a comment reminding me I always hated Wednesdays.

EXPECTED DEATH

When he couldn't argue back or challenge me, he ceased to be my dad. Then he was an empty shell, skin and bone and shallow breath.

Is it easier to lose someone suddenly? Vibrant when you leave the house, yet lifeless on return.

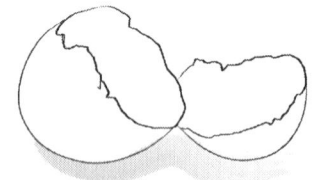

That way didn't seem easy at the time, but watching someone die is worse, isn't it?

'You get to say "goodbye" when it's expected' but I'm not sure if I did on that last afternoon as I left. Too much else going on. Other people in and out.

Even death that's expected never really goes to plan.

A FUNERAL IN COVID TIMES

One neighbour flies a flag at half-mast and people line the street as the cortege passes. Outside Dad's old butcher's shop, a cheer goes up that makes me cry. Others raise a glass outside the pub.

In ordinary times they would have packed the church, filling it with a celebration of life and love. The vast building looks strangely empty with limited mourners divided into smaller family groups.

Mum places the single rose from the garden on Dad's coffin.

I give the eulogy, confident my voice will not break and I can hold back the tears. I am proficient at standing up and delivering my well-crafted words. I count on my fingers how many times I have spoken at a funeral; a eulogy for Andrew was the first, then one for my nana, prayers for my aunt and a poem for Andrew's mum.

Afterwards as we spill out into the sunshine our emotions let rip with hugs and words of comfort we so desperately need to share, despite restrictions and rules. Dad was the baby of the family, the youngest of nine, just three of his siblings remain.

Only close family travel to the crem and afterwards, at our private wake we watch one of dad's favourite films, Gladiator, and share an Indian takeaway which wouldn't have been his choice, but none of us wants to cook.

Like all strange days, this will be etched in our memories forever.

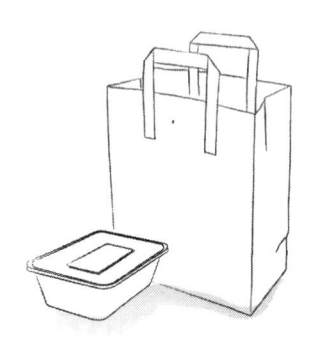

HAVE YOU EVER THOUGHT OF EXPLORING YOUR VOCATION?

I'm drifting, uncertain where I should be. I lost my compass years ago and now I've lost my anchor.

God should be my firm foundation but that rock is still crumbly; we don't always see eye to eye.

Other people try to nudge me and I've been pushed this way before, but I'm not sure I've been 'called'. God's one word to me has only ever been 'wait'!

Maybe I would have made a good vicar, perhaps I have the right attributes, skills and compassion.

Perhaps it is rebelliousness that puts me off, or the old-fashioned fear that I'm just not good enough.

And then there's a once heard, off-the-cuff comment that middle-aged women enter the ministry because they have nothing better to do.

I know I can make a difference without a dog collar; I have freedom to speak out with no restraints of convention or certain rules to adhere to.

And I can continue to spend months not talking to God if I choose, because I'm never certain if I am my own creation or the woman she actually wants me to be.

BACK ON THE STAGE

Cancer, chemo and Covid, a trifecta of C words stopped me in my tracks. So much for planning a new exciting life in my empty nest. This was supposed to be my time to fly too.

Then someone drops out of a new play written by a local drama group; I get my chance to be Len the caretaker. I could have changed the name to Leonora, a more feminine moniker to suit my own style, but I deliberately choose reinvention.

Asserting my own place in the town I grew up in, no longer identified solely as my father's daughter.

CRAZY GOLF FOR THREE

Once upon a time I could win every game we played together. Now it takes all my skill and concentration, but try as I might I can't compete.

For board games you both have better strategies than me, seeing several steps ahead. Your brains are sharper than mine ever was.

My hand-to-eye coordination for crazy golf has always been lacking, but today the laughter is infectious, the sun is shining and we celebrate another graduation. Just being together, in our tight-knit family of three.

I know that whatever we have lost, I have won the greatest prize.

ANNIVERSARY MORNING

I didn't bring two mugs of tea up to bed this morning. Just an Earl Grey for me. The quilt is humped up, almost person-shaped, but it's only pillows built up as a defence against my loneliness.

Back in bed, I take a sip of tea. Feeling inspired, I exchange the mug for a notebook and pen from the bedside table – the one you chose for me, to match the rest of the bedroom furniture when we married. It has a pull-out shelf to accommodate an entire breakfast tray, but my lone mug rests easily among books and pens.

ANGRY GHOSTS

Are you a ghost, unhappy with your lot? Misrepresented throughout history, with an axe to grind?

The premise taken by my friend is an interesting one. She has gathered imagined words from beyond the grave and turned them into poems.

Their words are ripe to be performed, and to promote her book she enlists our help to rant and rage upon the stage. I become Cleopatra, Marie Curie and Margaret Catchpole – a queen, a scientist and a horse thief.

Acting is most definitely required, dressing up is mandatory, and tea and cake is our reward at the WI meetings.

BATCH-COOKING BOLOGNESE

The kitchen is tiny but he hovers, trying to help. Finding utensils and pans; it is his kitchen so he knows where everything lives.

He grates a carrot while I stir the pot. The assistance is welcome but not wholly necessary.

It is like a dance and I am leading. I should let go, relax, and allow him to take over.

But I am Mum, always have been and always will be.

I dream of the day when he will cook for me without my hindrance. I will be swept along in the moment. A proper guest at his table.

HOPE

The search for glitter is never-ending, in January I look for snowdrops, demure and bashful. Once I had a garden full of them, today only a few survive having been transplanted, first to my dad's garden and now to mine. I wish they were bolder, less subtle, not hidden. Today I need to see them, in the same way as on rainy days I need to find a rainbow. We all need hope on difficult days and they creep up with unannounced regularity. There are tulips on the mantlepiece, bright purple supermarket flowers, who says money can't buy hopefulness?

IT'S A MIRACLE

The school hall is just the same as all those years ago when I was here the first time around. This is place where I did country dancing, performed Mull of Kintyre on the guitar, was a brother in the school production of *Joseph*.

Today we are doing a school assembly and I am the lame man, dejected and cast aside waiting at the gate begging for a few coins to eke out a living.

The story is familiar and today I act it out with added gusto. The disciples have no money to give but instead give me the power of God and tell me to walk. A miracle is the last thing the man expected, I scoff at the bold claims then I stand on faltering Bambi legs, wobble, and make the children laugh.

Then I practise walking, leaping and dancing as they laugh some more.

The sound of their joy fills me with glitter and I sparkle.

THE SIX PIECES OF JEWELLERY YOU BOUGHT ME

First an engagement ring, two sparkling diamonds and a crystal blue sapphire.

A wedding band naturally followed.

On our honeymoon you bought me pearls; on the birth of our children, a locket and an eternity ring.

I persuaded you to buy me a pair of earrings for my fortieth; I lost one soon after I turned fifty.

The chain on the locket had broken long ago; pearls are just not suitable for every day.

Most rings sit in a box at the back of a drawer; my wedding ring nestled perfectly inside yours.

But eternity is forever on my right ring finger.

Lost glitter in my hand all along.

ACKNOWLEDGEMENTS

When bad things happen so many people gather round and offer to help. The offers are genuinely expressed but inevitably some friends fall away, situations change, people move away. I am grateful to everyone who reached out to me when Andrew died and more recently when I had cancer.

If you know me and find yourself in this book, thank you for adding to my story. And if you are not in these pages, it does not mean you have not been important, I could have carried on writing these stories for years. If you have ever shared a cup of tea and cake at my kitchen table, if I have ever cried on your shoulder, if you have walked any part of the way on this journey with me, I want to thank you.

Forgive me for cheating and grouping people together so I don't inadvertently miss anyone out, my heartfelt thanks go to…

Church friends from Emmanuel Saltburn, Redcar Baptist Church, and St Mary's Hadleigh. Your love and prayers have sustained us.

Friday Tea friends – I love you more than I can say, the friendship we shared will last forever and certainly shaped the lives of my boys.

The Monday morning walking group, I never wrote you a story but I wrote you two poems, including one about knickers and if anyone has a copy of that please send it to me. The laughter we shared was priceless. I always look forward to joining you when I can, even if I struggle to keep up these days.

The Saltburn Writers' Group, who have gently encouraged and supported me to become the writer I am today – the only good thing to come out of the pandemic was Zoom meetings and being able to join you online each month is a gift.

The Suffolk Writer's Facebook group set up by Mai Black, thank you for giving me the chance to perform as one of your Angry Ghosts.

I am also indebted to another Suffolk writer Ruth Leigh, thank you for introducing me to all sorts of new writing ventures including inviting me to join Resolute Books. To all the Resolute writers I look forward to our continued collaboration.

Thanks to Sheila Jacobs for copy editing and Liz Carter for formatting – this book would be such a mess without your diligence and attention to detail.

And a big thank you to Rose Nicholson-Lewis (Olivia Rose Design) for the beautiful cover design and additional artwork.

Writing this book has taken many years and it has only got over the finish line due to help from the marvellous Stephanie Butland, who I first met over ten years ago when she led a writing workshop on turning a blog into a memoir. I was so naïve back then I thought this would be so much easier! Thank you for pushing me to dig deep, there were more tears shed in these last few months than have come out in a long time but my writing is all the better for it.

And finally thank you to Joe and Ben, always referred to as oldest son and youngest son in my blog because I did not want to embarrass you. You have grown into fine young men and I am immensely proud of you. A little bit of embarrassment at this stage won't hurt!

BIOGRAPHY

Sarah Nicholson grew up in the small market town of Hadleigh, Suffolk. In her mid-twenties, she moved to the northeast coast where she met and married Andrew. They had two sons.

When Andrew died unexpectedly aged 48, Sarah started blogging. Over the years she has unravelled, re-ravelled and is currently searching for lost glitter… the sparkly memories and delights that help her through the darkest of days.

In 2018, when both boys left home, Sarah moved back to Hadleigh, expecting to start an exciting new chapter of her life. Instead, she was diagnosed with cancer and went through chemotherapy. Then Covid turned the whole world upside down.

The search for lost glitter continues…

unravelling-edges.blogspot.com

re-ravelling.blogspot.com

insearchoflostglitter.blogspot.com

About Resolute Books

We are an independent press representing a consortium of experienced authors, professional editors and talented designers producing engaging and inspiring books of the highest quality for readers everywhere. We produce books in a number of genres including historical fiction, crime suspense, young adult dystopia, memoir, Cold War thrillers, and even Jane Austen fan fiction!

Find out more at resolutebooks.co.uk

for the joy of reading

Printed in Great Britain
by Amazon